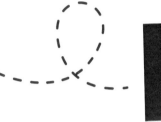

English Code 1

Grammar Book

Contents

Welcome!

1  **Watch. Underline the three names.**

Alexander: Hello! I'm Alexander.

Sara: Hello! I'm Sara!

Alexander: This is Polly. Say "Hello" Polly.

Polly: Hello, Polly!

2  **Watch again. Check for Polly.**

1 Say "Hello." ☐

2 Open the door. ☐

3 Sit down. ☐

3 **Read and match the opposites.**

CODE CRACKER

1 Sit down. •—   • a Close your book.

2 Open your book. •—   • b Put down your pencil.

3 Pick up your pencil. •— • c Stand up.

Language lab 1

OPEN YOUR BOOK

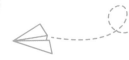

I will learn how to follow instructions in English.

1 Read and chant. Circle two actions.

Good morning, class.
Open your books.
It's time to learn.
Read. Listen. Write!
Read. Listen. Write!
It's time to learn.

Goodbye, class.
Close your books.
It's time to go home.
Close your books.
Close your books.
It's time to go home.

2 Read again. Underline *read* in blue. Underline *open* in red.

Open your books.   Read.

Close your books.   Write.

3 Read and match.

1   Listen.

2   Write.

3   Read.

a

b

c

4 Play *Teddy Says* with a partner. Say and act.

Close your book.   Listen.   Open your book.   Read.   Sit down.   Write.

4

Language lab 2

I'M / SHE'S ...

I will learn how to introduce myself.

1 Read and chant. Complete the sentence below.

Hi, I'm Jack. Nice to meet you.
What's your name? Are you new?
My name is Anna. It's great to meet you.
Hi, Anna. Welcome to our school.

She's Maria. She's at our school, too.
Hi, Anna. It's nice to meet you.
I'm eight. How old are you?
That's funny, Jack, I'm eight, too!

Jack is _____ .

2 Read again. Circle is and 's.

What**'s** your name?   How old **are** you?

I**'m** Jack.   I**'m** eight.

She**'s** Maria. / He**'s** Jack.   She**'s** eight. / He**'s** eight.

This **is** Polly.

3 Read and complete.

are   is   She's   your

1   This _____ Polly.

2   How old _____ you?

3   What's _____ name?

4   This is Sara. _____ eight.

4 Introduce yourself to a partner.

Hi! I'm Ben! How old are you?

Hi! I'm Lily! I'm seven.

5

1 Let's play!

1 ▶ Watch. Check ☑ the toys below.

airplane ☐	boat ☐	building blocks ☐	
doll ☐	octopus ☐	train ☐	

2 Read and complete. Then match.

It's   this   What's

1 **Alexander:** What's this?
   Sara: I know! _____ a train.
   Alexander: Yes! •—

2 **Alexander:** _____ this?
   Sara: It's an octopus!
   Alexander: Yes! •—

3 **Alexander:** What's _____ ?
   Sara: It's a boat.
   Alexander: Yes! •—

a

b

c

3 Look and draw. Then say.

CODE CRACKER

1 🔴 🧸 🔴 🧸 ☐
2 🚗 🔴 ✈️ 🚗 🔴 ☐
3 🚗 🧸 🧸 🚗 🧸 ☐

It's an airplane!

It's a ball!

It's a teddy bear!

6

Language lab 1

IT'S A / AN ...

> I will name toy words using **It's a / It's an.**

1 Read and look. What toys can you see?

_____   _____   _____   _____

Terrific Toys

Come and see our fantastic toys!
Boats! Dolls! Teddy bears! Toys for everyone!

It's an airplane.
It's yellow.

It's a teddy bear.
It's brown.

It's a doll.
It's big.

It's a boat.
It's small.

2 Read again. Underline it's in the text.

What's this?

It's a doll.

It's an airplane.

What is
= What's

It is
= It's

3 Read and complete.

doll   It's   this   What's

1 _____ a boat.

2 What's _____ ?

3 It's a _____ .

4 _____ this?

4 Look at the toys in your book. Point to them. Ask and answer with a partner.

What's this?

It's an airplane.

Language lab 2

IT'S A BIG / SMALL ...

1 Read and match.

1 It's a blue boat.

2 It's a black ball.

3 It's a black and white panda.

4 It's a blue bus.

What's this?
It's a **blue** doll.
It's a **big** car.

2 Read the sentences. Underline the words which describe things.

1 It's a big car.
2 It's a small building block.
3 It's a red doll.
4 It's a green train.

3 Look and write. Use It's.

1 It's an orange car. _____

2 _____ .

3 _____ .

4 _____ .

Language lab 1 and 2

1 Choose a word from each box and draw on paper. Let a partner guess.

| big   blue |
| pink   red |
| small   yellow |

| airplane   building blocks |
| car   doll   teddy bear |
| train |

> It's a yellow train.

> No, sorry! It's a red car.

2 Think about your favorite toy. Tell a partner.

> What's this, John?

> It's my favorite toy. It's a toy train. It's green. It's a green toy train.

3 Write about the toy.

My favorite toy

2 Art Club!

1 ▷ Watch. Circle.

1   (one pencil sharpener) / two pencil sharpeners
2   (five crayons) / six crayons
3   (three glue sticks) / four glue sticks

2 ▷ Read and match. Watch to check.

1   There's a •——   • a   sharpener.
2   There are •——   • b   ruler.
3   There are seven •——   • c   six crayons.
4   There is a pencil •——   • d   markers.

🇬🇧 British	🇺🇸 American
colouring pen	marker

3 Look at the table. Add two more words.

CODE CRACKER

There is ...	There are ...
a ruler.	two rulers.
a pen.	three pens.

Language lab 1

THERE IS / ARE …

1 Read and look. What's the name of the teacher?

**New Art Club on Tuesdays.
Come along and have fun!**

There is one teacher – Mrs. Lopez.

There are pencils. There are glue sticks.

There are paints.

Time to have fun!

See you there!

The teacher is _____ .

2 Complete. Use is or are.

1   There _____ one teacher.
2   There _____ six pens.
3   There _____ a glue stick.
4   There _____ two crayons and
    four erasers.
5   There _____ three paintbrushes
    and ten pencil cases.

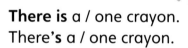

There is a / one crayon.
There's a / one crayon.

There are two crayons.

There are three erasers
and two glue sticks.

3 Look at the picture for one minute. Cover. Write on paper. Then check with a partner.

There is one ruler.

Language lab 2

HOW MANY ...?

*I will ask about art items using **How many**.*

1 Read and look. Label the items in bold.

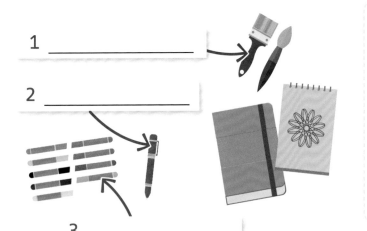

1 _____

2 _____

3 _____

4 _____

Hi, I'm Megan. I love Art! This is my desk. How many pencils are there? Hmm ... one, two, three, four ... There are ten pencils! There is one **pen** and there are notebooks. There are **crayons**. There are **paint pots** and **paintbrushes**, too. The paintbrushes are big!

How many rulers **are** there?

There is one ruler.

There are four ruler**s**.

There are two blue ruler**s and** two yellow ruler**s**.

2 Look again. Match the questions and answers.

1 How many crayons are there? ●—
2 How many pens are there? ●—
3 How many paint pots are there? ●—
4 How many paintbrushes are there? ●—

●a There is one.
●b There are nine.
●c There are two.
●d There are ten.

3 Read and complete.

are   is   There (×2)

1 How many pencils _____ there?   2 _____ is one eraser.

3 _____ are nine crayons.   4 There _____ a pen.

Language lab 1 and 2

1 Look at the picture. Order the words.

1 How many   there?   are   pencils

_____

2 there?   are   How many   erasers

_____

3 glue sticks   there?   are   How many

_____

4 crayons   are   How many   there?

_____

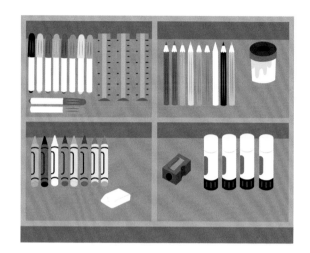

2 Look at 1. Write the answers.

1 There are nine pencils.

2 _____ .

3 _____ .

4 _____ .

3 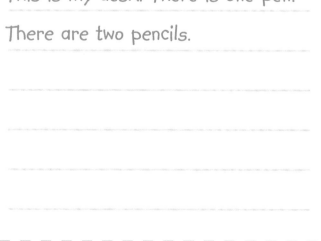 Draw items on the desk. Write about them.

This is my desk. There is one pen.

There are two pencils.

_____

_____

_____

_____

3 Families

1 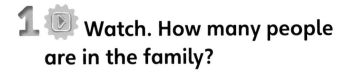 **Watch. How many people are in the family?**

> five   nine   ten

2 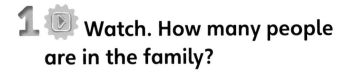 **Read and complete. Watch to check.**

> his   my (×2)   your

1   Sara — This is _____ cousin, Pedro.

2   Sara — Ana is _____ sister.

3   Sara — This is _____ brother, Alexander.

4   Alexander — Yes! I'm _____ brother, Sara.

3 **You are Alexander. Match.**

CODE CRACKER

1   Pedro is my ...

2   Ana is my ...

3   Sara is my ...

a   cousin

b   sister

c   cousin

Language lab 1

THIS IS MY / YOUR / HIS / HER

> I will introduce my family using **This is**.

1 Read and answer T (True) or F (False) for Harry.

Rebecca: Hi, Harry. Is this your photo?

Harry: Yes, it is. This is my family.
They live in Mexico.

Rebecca: Cool. Who's this?

Harry: This is my cousin, Luis. And this is his sister, Ava.
This is their dad, my uncle Francisco.

Rebecca: Great. Who's this?

Harry: This is my aunt, Véronica.
And this is her mom and dad.

Rebecca: Are they your grandma
and grandpa?

Harry: Yes, they are. They're lovely.

Rebecca: Thanks.

1	Luis is his cousin.	T / F
2	Véronica is his grandma.	T / F
3	Ava is his dad.	T / F

I am Tom. → This is **my** dad.

Hi, Debbie. → This is **your** mom.

He is Henry. → This is **his** brother.

This is Zoe. → This is **her** sister.

🇬🇧 British	🇺🇸 American
mum	mom

2 Look and match.

1 his ●   ● a ♀

2 her ●   ● b ♂

3 my ●   ● c ♀

3 Look and write.

her   his   my

This is _____ grandpa.

This is _____ brother.

This is _____ mom.

15

Language lab 2

WHO ...?

*I will ask about family using **Who's this?***

1 Read and chant. Label the people in bold.

Who's this? Who's this?
This is my family and me.
Who's this? Who's this?
This is my grandma, **Stephanie**!

Who's this? Who's this?
This is my family and me.
Who's this? Who's this?
This is her brother, **Barnaby**!

Who's this? Who's this?
This is my family and me.
Who's this? Who's this?
This is our cousin, **Melanie**!

1 _____

2 _____

3 _____

She is Selena. ➔ This is **her** grandpa.

We are Mason and Mike. ➔ This is **our** grandpa.

They are Judy and Jill. ➔ This is **their** grandpa.

Who is this? /
Who's this?

2 Read and circle.

1 This / Who is this?

2 This / Who is my grandpa.

3 This is Sandra and this is
   her / his mom.

4 They are sisters. This is
   her / their pet dog.

5 We are sisters. This is Ryan.
   He is her / our friend.

3 Order the words. Make sentences.

1 my   is   This   grandma

   _____.

2 This   our   brother   is

   _____.

3 is   their   dad   This

   _____.

4 this   is   Who

   _____?

5 aunt   is   This   his

   _____.

16

Language lab 1 and 2

1 Read and circle.

1 Hi, Lee. Who's this? It's my / your brother.

2 Hello, Katie and Billy. Who's this? It's our / their mom.

3 Hello. This is my dad. And this is his / her brother.

4 Hi, Jason. Look. This is Pip, my / your cat.

5 Hello. This is my grandpa and this is my grandma.
   And this is our / their pet fish, Speedy.

2 Read the text. Ask and answer.

Hi, I'm Steven. I'm six. My family is small.
This is my brother. His name is Noah.
He's fourteen. He's great. This is our mom.
Her name is Dina. This is our dad, Michael.
My parents are
cool. They're funny!
This is our dog. We
love our dog. Her
name is Bella. She's
six – the same
as me!

1 Who is Noah?

2 Who is Dina?

3 Who is Bella?

4 Who is Michael?

> Who is Noah?

> Noah is his brother.

> That's right!

3 Write about your family.

Puppet show!

1  **Watch. Look and write.**

girl   wolf

1 _____   2 _____

🇬🇧 **British**	🇺🇸 **American**
have got	have
has got	has

2 **Look, read, and circle. Watch to check.**

1 He has / have a big nose and big eyes.

2 She has / have small eyes.

3 **Sara:** I has / have a big mouth.

3  **Number the story in order.**

CODE CRACKER ⚙️⚙️⚙️

_____   _____   _____

Language lab 1

I / YOU HAVE AND HE / SHE HAS

1 Read. Underline the body parts.

Your Body

Do you have eight or ten toes? Find out with Doctor Louisa!

Our bodies are amazing! You have one head. I have one head, too. I have black hair. I'm Doctor Louisa, and I'm just like you!

You have two strong arms and two hands. You have five fingers on each hand. They are good for drawing.

You have two feet. You have five toes on each foot. They are good for climbing.

You have two eyes, one mouth, one nose, and two ears.

You have two strong legs. One leg, two legs. They are good for playing soccer!

one **foot** → two **feet**

2 Look and circle.

1 I have / has big eyes.
2 You have / has small feet.
3 She have / has black hair.
4 He have / has ten toes.
5 You have / has long arms.

I **have** ten toes.
You **have** two arms.
He **has** two eyes.
She **has** black hair.

3 Write about you. Then write about a family member.

Me	My _____
1 I have _____ hair.	1 _____ .
2 I have _____ eyes.	2 _____ .
3 I have _____ .	3 _____ .
4 I have _____ .	4 _____ .

19

Language lab 2

I'M / YOU'RE / HE'S / SHE'S

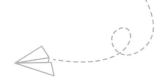
I will describe height using **I'm** / **You're** / **He's** / **She's**.

1 Read and chant. Who has brown hair?

I'm short, you're tall. You're my brother, Ben.
I'm only seven. You are big – you're ten!

You have brown eyes. I have blue eyes.
This is my brother. He's a different size!

I'm short, you're tall. You're my brother, Ben.
I'm only seven. You are big – you're ten!

You have brown hair. I have blond hair.
Where are you now? Oh, you're up there!

I'm short, you're tall. You're my brother, Ben.
I'm only seven. You are big – you're ten!

_____ **has brown hair.**

Poppy   Ben

2 Read again. Underline 'm, 's and 're.

3 Read and match.

1 He is
2 You are
3 I am
4 She is

a She's
b I'm
c You're
d He's

I'm tall.	=	I am tall.
You're short.	=	You are short.
He's short.	=	He is short.
She's tall.	=	She is tall.

4 Write the missing letters.

1 He'_____ tall.   2 S_____'s short.

3 I'_____ eight.   4 Y_____'re seven.

Language lab 1 and 2

1 Read and complete.

am   has   have   He's   is

Hi, I'm Sam and I 1 _____ seven. I 2 _____ a small family. My mom 3 _____ short. Her name is Gloria. She 4 _____ big eyes. My dad is tall. He has black hair. He has big feet! His name is Daniel. I have a pet cat, too. His name is Scooter. 5 _____ gray and brown. He's so cute!

2 Draw your family. Then tell a partner. Use these words.

This is my family. I have a …

Eyes: blue, green, brown

Hair: long, short

Height: tall, short

My Family.

3 Describe someone in your family in 2. Let a partner guess who it is.

He's short. He has brown hair.

Yes, that's right!

Your brother, Max!

5 The perfect pet

1 ▷ **Watch. Circle Alexander's favorite animals.**

birds   cats   dogs   rabbits

2 ▷ **Choose T (True) or F (False). Watch to check.**

1 The rabbit can hop.   T / F
2 Mittens the cat can't run.   T / F
3 Mittens the cat can climb.   T / F
4 Polly can't fly.   T / F

3 Circle the odd one out. Then match.

CODE CRACKER

1 dog   bird   cat   rabbit •   • a   It can swim.
2 cat   fish   lizard   mouse •   • b   It can hop.
3 rabbit   horse   dog   cat •   • c   It can fly.

Language lab 1

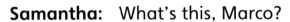

> I will talk about actions using **can** and **can't**.

1 Read and answer. Can Mr. Amazing fly?

_____

Samantha:	What's this, Marco?
Marco:	It's a new comic! It's about Mr. Amazing. He can run.
Samantha:	I can run, too!
Marco:	He can swim.
Samantha:	I can swim, too!
Marco:	He can fly! This is his super dog, Speedy. He can fly too!
Samantha:	Wow. I can …
Marco:	You can't fly, Sam!
Samantha:	No, you're right. I can run, but I can't fly!
Marco:	Ha ha.

> I **can** jump, **but** I **can't** swim.
>
> You **can't** climb, **but** you **can** run.
>
> He / She / It **can** hop, **but** he / she / it **can't** fly.

2 Read again. Underline *can* in blue and *can't* in red.

3 Read again and write T (True) or F (False).

1 Mr. Amazing can run. _____

2 Samantha can swim. _____

3 Samantha can run. _____

4 Mr. Amazing can't fly. _____

5 Samantha can fly. _____

6 Speedy the super dog can fly. _____

4 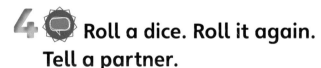 Roll a dice. Roll it again. Tell a partner.

1 run
2 jump
3 swim
4 fly
5 hop
6 climb

> It's a 2! And it's a 3! I can jump, but I can't swim.

Language lab 2

WE CAN / THEY CAN'T

1 **Read. What pets are there? Choose.**

My Perfect Pets

Hi, I'm Kylie. I have three pets. They can do a lot of things. They can all run.

I have a pet rabbit. Her name is Lucky. She can't jump, but she can hop! She's old. She hops slowly. I have a dog, too. His name is Colin. He can run quickly. He can swim too, but he can't hop. I can't hop either!

I have a cat – Charlie. He's only one. He's very cute. He's never tired. I love my pets! We can play in the garden together.

a a bird, a fish, and a rabbit

b a cat, a rabbit, and a fish

c a cat, a rabbit, and a dog

2 **Read again. Underline they and we. Circle how the animals do different things.**

3 **Order the words. Make sentences.**

I / You	can	run	quickly.
He / She / It	can't		slowly.
We / They			

1 run   We   quickly   can

_____ .

2 can't   run   They   slowly

_____ .

3 She   quickly   swim   can

_____ .

4 He   swim   can't   quickly

_____ .

4 💬 **Check for you. Then complete for two partners.**

	Me	P1	P2
Run quickly			
Run slowly			
Swim quickly			
Swim slowly			

I can run quickly.

Me too!

Language lab 1 and 2

1 Read and complete.

can   can't   climb   run   quickly

Hamsters

Hamsters are popular pets in the UK. They are small and cute. They can be white, brown, or orange. They can 1 _____ and jump. They can run but they 2 _____ swim.

Horses

Horses are big pets. This horse is in Mexico. Horses are tall. They can be white, brown, orange, black, or gray. They can 3 _____ 4 _____. They 5 _____ even swim, too, but they can't fly!

2 Imagine this is your pet. Tell a partner.

This is my pet. It's a rabbit. Her name is Snowy. She can …

3 Write about your favorite pet.

_____

_____

_____

_____

_____

_____

6 Fruit bowl!

1 ▶ Watch. Label the fruit you can see.

2 ▶ Write sentences. Watch to check.

1 **Sara:** I 🙁 kiwis

I don't like kiwis.

2 **Alexander:** I 🙂 pears

_____ .

3 **Sara:** I 😃 watermelons

_____ .

4 **Alexander:** I 🙁 watermelons

_____ .

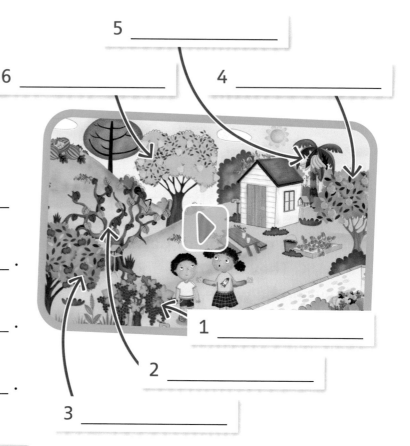

5 _____

6 _____   4 _____

1 _____

2 _____

3 _____

3 Order the letters to make fruit words. Complete the sentences.

CODE CRACKER

1	e a r p s	I like _____ .
2	i s i k w	You don't like _____ .
3	m w t e a r s l o n e	You like _____ .
4	p l p s a e	I don't like _____ .
5	g s o a n r e	I like _____ .

Language lab 1

I / WE / THEY LIKE / DON'T LIKE

> I will talk about what we **like** and **don't like**.

1 Read. Which fruit are in the chant?

_____   _____   _____   _____

Come on, come on! To the lemonade stand!
Where is it? I can show you. Take my hand!

What do you like? What do you like?
Lemonade, lemonade. I like lemonade!
I don't like oranges or apples, oh no!

Come on, come on! To the lemonade stand!
Where is it? I can show you. Take my hand!

What do you like? What do you like?
Lemonade, lemonade. We like lemonade!
I don't like pears or kiwis, oh no!

What **do** you **like**?

I / You **like** apples. 😃

We / They **don't like** apples. 😦

do not
= don't

2 Read again. Underline *like* in blue. Underline *don't like* in red.

3 Write the missing letters.

1 What _____ you like?

2 You l_____ strawberries.

3 I d_____ like bananas.

4 They _____n't like mangoes.

5 We _____ apples.

4 You are Sara. Your partner is Alexander. Role play.

	Alexander	Sara
😃	grapes, pears	grapes
😦	watermelons, kiwis	kiwis

Hi, Alexander. What do you like?

Hi, Sara. I like grapes and pears.

Language lab 2

HE / SHE LIKES / DOESN'T LIKE

1 Read and complete the sentences below.

Do you have questions about animals? Meet Andy the Vet!

Hi, Andy. Nice to meet you. I have a new pet rabbit. Her name is Shirley. What fruit does she like?

Well, your rabbit likes apples!

Oh. I like apples, too!

And I have a pet bird. His name is Sunny. What does he like?

He likes oranges.

I see! I have a cat, Kitty. She *doesn't* like apples!

That's right. Your cat doesn't like any fruit!

Poor Kitty!

> **What does** he like?
> He **likes** apples.
> She **doesn't like** apples.

1   The bird likes _____ .

2   The cat doesn't like _____ .

3   The rabbit likes _____ .

2 Read and match.

1   What does Alex like?
    He likes bananas. •

2   He doesn't like grapes. •

3   He doesn't like apples. •

a

b

c

3 Look and write.

1   She / ✓ / grapes

    _____ .

2   He / ✗ / oranges

    _____ .

3   She / ✗ / kiwis

    _____ .

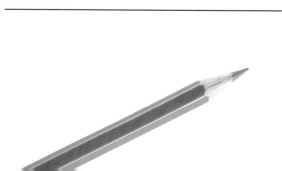

Language lab 1 and 2

1 Read and match.

1 What do •
2 I like •
3 He doesn't •
4 They like pears, but •
5 What •
6 We •

• a   does she like?
• b   don't like oranges.
• c   like grapes.
• d   you like?
• e   apples.
• f   they don't like watermelons.

2 Look and write the sentences.

Name: Ben

Age: seven

☺ : grapes, bananas, pineapples

☹ : oranges, apples, strawberries

1   His name is _____ and
    he _____ seven.
2   He _____ bananas.
3   He _____ grapes and
    _____ .
4   He _____ _____ oranges.
5   He _____ _____ apples.

3 Make a fruit poster. Swap with a partner. Tell the class about your new poster.

My favorite fruit

_____
_____

Fruit I don't like

_____
_____

Hi, I'm Nikki. This is my new poster.
I like apples and … I don't like …

7 Let's get active

1 ▶ Watch. Check ☑ or cross ☒ .

climb   climb   paint   hop

2 ▶ Read and complete. Watch to check.

do   don't   draw   play

🇬🇧 British	🇺🇸 American
play football	play soccer

1 **Sara:** I _____ climb and I don't run.

2 **Alexander and Sara:** We _____ soccer in the afternoon.

3 **Sara:** I don't paint, but I _____ .

4 **Alexander:** What _____ we do in the evening?

3 Read and complete.

CODE CRACKER ⚙⚙⚙

	in the morning	in the afternoon	in the evening
Sara	I hop.	We 1 _____ soccer and we play music.	We 3 _____ home.
Alexander	I run.	We 2 _____ soccer and we play music.	We 4 _____ home.

Language lab 1

I / YOU / WE / THEY SWIM / DON'T SWIM

> I will ask about hobbies using action words.

1 Read. How many activities are there in the text?

Dan's blog

I'm Dan. I'm seven. I am an active kid! At school,
I paint and I draw. It's fun! I play soccer, too. It's fun!
I don't swim. I don't like it.

At home, I ride a bike and play music. I play with
my sister. We play the piano together. I like music,
but I don't sing! What activities do you do?

_____ activities

2 Read again. You are Dan. Circle.

1 At school, I paint / don't paint .

2 At home, I sing / don't sing .

> **What** activities do you **do**?
> I / We **paint**. ✓
> You / They **don't** play soccer. ✗

3 Look and write the sentences.

1 We _____ *play soccer* _____ .

2 You _____ .

3 They _____ .

4 What activities do you do? Ask and answer.

What activities do you do?

I can climb and sing. I don't draw.

Language lab 2

HE / SHE SINGS / DOESN'T SING

I will ask about actions using **What does...?**

1 Read. What does Daria do?

_____.

Amazing Acrobats!

Come and see Darius and Daria!

This is my cousin, Darius. And this is my cousin, Daria. They are acrobats! They're amazing!
Darius rides a bike. He runs quickly! He doesn't sing. He doesn't dance. Daria is his sister. She climbs. She jumps. She doesn't ride a bike. Daria and Darius are fantastic acrobats!

What activities **does** he / she **do**?

He dances. ✓

She **doesn't play** music. ✗

2 What's different? Underline.

1 He sings.   2 He doesn't sing.   3 She climbs.   4 She doesn't climb.

3 Look. Ask and answer.

play soccer ✓
paint ✓
swim ✗

climb ✓
read ✓
ride a bike ✗

What activities does she do?

She plays soccer.

Language lab 1 and 2

1 Read and circle.

1 I (play) / plays the piano.

2 He (swim) / swims in the pool.

3 We (climb) / climbs trees.

4 What activities (do) / does he do?

5 We (don't) / doesn't paint.

6 He (don't) / doesn't play soccer.

7 You (dance) / dances at school.

8 They (read) / reads at home.

2 Look and write for you.

In the park	At school	At home
ride a bike 	read 	play soccer 
read	swim	read
climb	paint	draw

I climb, *but* I
don't ride a bike.

In the park I ride a bike, but I don't read.

_____

_____

3 How many questions and answers can you make?
You can use words more than once.

What   she   sing   do   does   climb

we   activities   dance   do   doesn't   climb

What does she do?   She dances.

_____

_____

_____

8 Let's dress up

1 ▶ Watch. What clothes do you hear? Check ☑.

1 socks ☐   2 sweater ☐

3 hat ☐   4 skirt ☐

2 ▶ Watch again. Complete, then draw.

①   **②**   **③**   **④**

1 sweater _____ my bag

2 teddy bear _____ my bag

3 shoes _____ the table

4 train _____ the table

🇬🇧 British	🇺🇸 American
jumper	sweater

3 Look and complete the sequence.

CODE CRACKER

1 red shoes, red dress, yellow shoes, _____ _____ _____

2 green socks, blue dress, green dress, _____ _____ _____

3 purple hat, pink skirt, purple hat, _____ _____ _____

Language lab 1

IN, ON, AND UNDER

I will talk about where clothes are using **in**, **on**, and **under**.

1 Read. What is in the box?

_____ .

Mom: OK, Rosie. It's tidy up time now!

Rosie: OK, Mom. First, the building blocks.

Mom: Great, thanks. The building blocks are all in the box.

Rosie: Now, the dolls! The dolls are under the table.

Mom: Oh dear! That's right, Rosie. Now the dolls are in the box.

Rosie: Mom, the train is on the table.

Mom: Now it's in the box.

Rosie: Here's a ball. It's under a chair.

Mom: Here is a hat. It's on the chair.

Rosie: Let's put it them both in the box.

Mom: Great job, Rosie! The box is full now!

The ball is **under** the box.

The ball is **on** the box.

The ball is **in** the box.

under   on   in

2 Where do Rosie and her mom look? Read again and check ✓.

on the chair ☐

on the table ☐

in the bag ☐

in the box ☐

under the chair ☐

under the table ☐

3 Read again. Underline on, in, and under.

4 Look around the room. Find two of these things. Make sentences.

glue stick   pencils
pencil case   pens   ruler

The glue stick is on the table.

1 _____

_____ .

2 _____

_____ .

Language lab 2

WHERE IS / WHERE ARE ...?

I will ask where clothes are using **Where ...?**

1 Read and chant. Circle two items of clothes.

Time to get ready! It's disco time.
Where is my pink hat? Is it here or there?
Oh, here it is! It's on the chair.
Time to get ready! It's disco time.

Time to get ready! It's disco time.
Where are my black shoes? Are they here or there?
Oh, here they are! They're under the table.
Time to get ready! It's disco time.

Where is my hat?   It **is** / It**'s** under the chair.

Where are my shoes?   They **are** / They**'re** under the chair.

2 Read again. Underline questions with *Where is* in green. Underline questions with *Where are* in orange.

3 Look, read, and complete. Then circle T (True) or F (False).

1 **A:** _____ is my sweater?   T / F

   B: It's under the bag.

2 **A:** _____ are my shoes?   T / F

   B: They're under the table.

3 **A:** _____ _____ my shorts?   T / F

   B: They're under the chair.

4 Look at the pictures in 3. Ask and answer.

Where is the sweater?   It's in the bag.

Language lab 1 and 2

1 Read and complete.

are   in   is   where

David: Mom! Where 1 _____ my hat?

Mom: Let's see … It's under your table!

David: Thanks, Mom. And 2 _____ is my T-shirt?

Mom: It's here. It's on your chair!

David: Thanks, Mom. Where 3 _____ my pants?

Mom: Look. Your pants are 4 _____ the bag.

David: Great, thanks, Mom. I'm ready now!

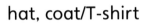

2 Choose a costume. Write a short dialog.

blue T-shirt/black mask

hat, coat/T-shirt

3 Act out your dialog with a partner.

Extra Grammar 1

IT'S A / AN ...

I will identify an object using **a** or **an**.

1 Read and chant. Circle the things that start with *a* and *o*.

My Silly Chant

An **apple** is great. An **apple** is sweet.
A pear is yummy, better than my feet!

Eyes are big and round. They're in my head.
An eye is closed. It's time for bed!

A chocolate cake. Yum, yum, yum.
An **ice cream** cone is so tasty. Thanks, Mom!

A dolphin, an **octopus**. They live in the sea.
An **octopus** has eight legs – six more than me!

A grandpa is kind. An **uncle** is great.
I love my family. My sister is Kate!

> It's **an a**pple.
>
> It's **a b**ook.
>
> **An o**range is delicious.
>
> **A p**ear is yummy.
>
> There is **an e**raser on my table.
>
> There is **a p**en on the desk.

2 Sort the words.

aunt   cat   eraser
glue stick   orange
pencil case

A	AN

3 Read the sentences. Choose *a* or *an*.

1   It's (a) / an pencil.

2   There is (a) / an apple.

3   (A) / An ice cream is tasty.

4   It's (a) / an orange pencil case.

5   There is (a) / an rabbit in the park.

38

Extra Grammar 2

HOW OLD IS / ARE ...?

> I will ask and answer about how old I am.

1 Read and look. Who is the birthday girl?

Jordan: Hi Tia. How are you?

Tia: Good, thanks. Look at my photo!

Jordan: Who is that?

Tia: It's my sister, Gracie. It's her birthday.

Jordan: How old is she?

Tia: She's eight.

Jordan: And how old are her friends?

Tia: They're eight, too. They're all the same age now!

_____ is the birthday girl.

2 Complete the questions.

> How   How   is   old

> How old are you?
> I am six.   I'm six.
> How old is he / she?
> He is / She is six.   He's / She's six.
> How old are they?
> They are eight.   They're eight.

1 _____ old are you?

2 How old _____ he?

3 _____ _____ are they?

3 Ask and answer about these people. Then ask and answer about you.

> How old is she?

> She's ...

Extra Grammar 3

THIS / THAT CAR, THESE / THOSE TRAINS

I will identify objects using **this / that / these / those**.

1 Read and look. What toy does Bradley choose?

Mom:	OK, Bradley. Let's buy a present for Tom. It's his birthday.
Bradley:	OK, Mom.
Shop assistant:	Can I help you?
Bradley:	We need a toy for my friend.
Shop assistant:	OK. This is a nice robot.
Bradley:	Yes …
Shop assistant:	And that is a yellow train.
Bradley:	Maybe …
Shop assistant:	What about building blocks? Those building blocks are red.
Bradley:	I like them, but …
Shop assistant:	OK, I know! Look here.
Bradley:	These cars are great! Let's have these!

2 Read again. Underline this, that, these, and those.

3 Read and choose.

1 This is a car / cars .
2 This / These are the building blocks.
3 These are my train / trains .
4 That / Those is a nice doll.

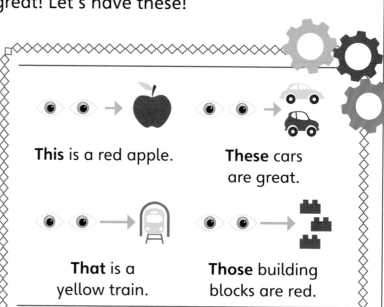

This is a red apple.

These cars are great.

That is a yellow train.

Those building blocks are red.

4. Look and match. Then complete.

those   that

a

b

1 **Girl:** Wow, _____ robot is cool!

2 **Man:** _____ are colorful balls!

🇬🇧 British	🇺🇸 American
colourful	colorful

5 Read and write this, that, these, or those.

1 _____ are my favorite building blocks!

2 _____ is my favorite teddy!

3 _____ are yummy cakes!

4 _____ is a duck!

6. Draw toys in a toy store. Then write four sentences about them with this or that.

That is a red car.

_____

_____

_____

Extra Grammar 4

I PLAY WITH YOU / HIM / HER / IT / THEM; PLAY WITH ME / US

I will identify people using **me, you, him, her.**

1 Read and underline the toys in the text.

Look at me! Look at me! I'm here with my toys!
Look at me! Look at me! I'm here with girls and boys!
Let's play with blocks! Let's ask Will and Tim.
And what about George? Let's go and ask him.

Look at me! Look at me! I'm here with my toys!
Look at me! Look at me! I'm here with girls and boys!
Do you like my new blue car? You can play with it.
Do you like my new green doll? Look at her. She sits!

Look at me! Look at me! I'm here with my toys!
Look at me! Look at me! I'm here with girls and boys!
I really love your trains. Can I play with them?
Oh no, playtime's over! No more time!

2 Read again. Match the sentences from the chant.

1 Look at
2 You can play with
3 Let's go and ask

a it.
b him.
c her.

3 Read again. Underline the words me, them, her, it, him.

I	→	Look at **me**.	We	→	You can play with **us**.
You	→	I can see **you**.	You	→	I can see **you**.
He	→	Let's go and ask **him**.	They	→	Can I play with **them**?
She	→	Look at **her**.			
It	→	You can play with **it**.			

4 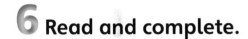 Look at the bold words in the grammar box on page 42. Where are they in the sentence?

a   at the beginning

b   in the middle

c   at the end

5 Read and circle the correct picture.

1   I like her.

2   Let's ask him.

3   I like it.

4   She plays with them.

6 Read and complete.

her   it   them   us

I'm Rocco. Here are my toys. They are toy trains. I like 1 _____ . They are red, green, and yellow. I have a robot, too. I love 2 _____ . It's my favorite toy.

I'm Lee. I play with my sister, Penny. Penny is funny. I love 3 _____ . We have a mom and dad. We have a grandma and grandpa, too. They love 4 _____ very much.

7 Write about your toys or family. Use it/him/her/them.

I'm Charlie. I love my toys. This is my favorite airplane. It's blue. I love it!

_____

_____

Grammar Reference

Unit 1

Language lab 1

Simple present with *it's*:

What's this?
It's a doll.

What's this?
It's a window.

Determiners + noun:

What's this?
It's *a* book.

What's this?
It's *an* octopus.

Language lab 2

Determiners + adjective + noun:

What's this?
It's a *red* door.

What's this?
It's a *big* chair.

What's this?
It's an *orange* teddy bear.

What's this?
It's a *small* table.

Unit 2

Language lab 1

***There's/There are* + conjunction *and*:**

There's a boat.
There's a ball.
There are three cars *and* two buses.

Language lab 2

***How many ... are there*?**
There is/are ...

How many boats *are there*?
There is one boat.

How many trains *are there*?
There are two trains.

How many airplanes *are there*?
There are four airplanes.

Unit 3

Language lab 1

Possessive adjectives:

This is *my* cousin.
This is *your* grandpa.
This is *his* aunt.
This is *her* sister.

Language lab 2

***Who's* + possessive adjectives:**

Who's this?
This is *my* mom.

Who's this?
This is *his* sister.

Who's this?
This is *your* uncle.

Who's this?
This is *her* baby.

Unit 4

Language lab 1

***has/have*:**

I *have* small feet.
You *have* green eyes.
He *has* big ears.
She *has* red hair.

Language lab 2

***be* verb:**

I'm short.   *He's* short.
You're tall.   *She's* tall.

Grammar Reference

Unit 5

Language lab 1

I/You/He/She/It can/can't

I *can* run.   You *can* swim.

He *can't* climb.   She *can't* fly.

It *can't* hop.

Conjunction: *but*

I *can* run *but* I *can't* fly.

He *can* fly *but* he *can't* climb.

Language lab 2

We/They can + verb + adverb

We can swim *quickly*.
They can't hop *slowly*.

Unit 6

Language lab 1

What do you *like*?
I/We/They *like/don't like* ...

What do you *like*?
I *like* apples. I *don't like* kiwis.
We *like* grapes. We *don't like*
pineapples.

They *like* watermelons.
They *don't like* oranges.

Language lab 2

What does he/she *like*?
He/She *likes/doesn't like* ...

What does he *like*?
He *likes* pears. He *doesn't like*
mangoes.

What does she *like*?
She *likes* strawberries.
She *doesn't like* bananas.

Unit 7

Language lab 1

Simple Present:

**What activities do you do?
I …/I don't**

What activities do you do?
I *dance*. I *don't draw*.
You *sing*. You *don't play* soccer.
We *paint*. We *don't climb*.
They *draw*. They *don't run*.

Language lab 2

Simple Present (third person):

**What activities does he/she do?
He/She …/He/She doesn't …**

What activities does he do?
He *paints*. He *doesn't ride* a bike.

What activities does she do?
She *plays* music. She *doesn't swim*.

Unit 8

Language lab 1

Prepositions of place:

**The item(s) is/are (*in*, *on*, *under*)
the …**
The ruler is *in* the bag.
The glue stick is *under* the chair.
The crayons are *on* the table.
The cat is *on* the books.

Language lab 2

**Where *is* …?
It *is* …**

**Where *are* …?
They *are* …**

Where *is* the paintbrush?
It is on the chair.

Where *are* the paint pots?
They are under the table.

Pearson Education Limited
KAO TWO
KAO Park
Hockham Way
Harlow, Essex
CM17 9SR
England

and Associated Companies throughout the world.

english.com/englishcode

First published 2021

Second impression 2024

ISBN: 978-1-292-32314-5

Set in Heinemann Roman 13.5pt

Printed in Slovakia by Neografia

Image Credit(s):

123RF.com: Aliaksei Luskin 6, anatols 32, Anutr Yossundara 7, 9, Cathy Yeulet 19, 39, Jozef Polc 31, luckybusiness 41, Oksana Kuzmina 37, Preve Beatrice 20, yganko 4, zayatssv 7, 9; **Alamy Stock Photo:** Marc Tielemans 6; **Getty Images:** Mima Foto / EyeEm 4, 17, 29; **Pearson Education Ltd:** Jon Barlow 5, 9, 21, Jules Selmes 43, Studio 8 4; **Shutterstock.com:** 76219 4, Africa Studio 31, AJR_photo 28, AlexKalashnikov 25, AM-STUDiO 7, 9, Andrew Burgess 6, 7, 9, Anna Photographer 10, 17, 33, Apollofoto 15, Cora Mueller 24, Creativa Images 4, 41, Danila 21, Dewald Kirsten 25, Digital Media Pro 32, Duplass 39, Emese 42, ESB Professional 29, 31, g-stockstudio 36, Ger Bosma Photos 38, Guryanov Andrey 32, Hurst Photo 27, Justin Kim 28, Kenishirotie 39, Lanski 31, Levent Konuk 37, Lukas Gojda 3, 4, 10, 17, 22, 28, 28, 29, 32, M. Unal Ozmen 38, Mariusz S. Jurgielewicz 31, Oleg Krugliak 31, Olesia Babushkina 39, Olga Gabay 37, Pavel L Photo and Video 40, Phase4Studios 9, Pimsdelamour 25, pixelheadphoto digitalskillet 15, Rob Hainer 17, Rob Marmion 15, 31, 41, Robnroll 38, Ruslan Guzov 31, Ruth Black 39, Sergey Novikov 19, Shutterstock 11, 15, 43, Syda Productions 5, 23, 41, Tatiana Popova 28, Tim UR 28, timquo 7, 20, 27, 37, 39, topseller 28, 38, Tracy Whiteside 32, Vladvm 38, wavebreakmedia 16

Animation screen shots

Artwork by Constanza Basaluzzo (MB Artists), production by Dardanele Studio

All other images © Pearson Education

Illustrated by Constanza Basaluzzo/MB Artists, pp. 3, 6, 8 (bottom), 10, 14, 18, 22, 26, 30, 34; Tim Bradford/Illustration Ltd, pp. 8 (top), 11, 13, 36, 44 (top), 46 (left); Richard Watson/Bright Agency, pp. 44 (bottom), 45, 46 (bottom right), 47.

Cover Image: *Front:* **Pearson Education Ltd:** Jon Barlow